MARRIAGE&DIVORCE

*An address given by
President Spencer W. Kimball
in the Marriott Center
at Brigham Young University
on September 7, 197*

*Published by
Deseret Book Company
Salt Lake City, Utah
197*

MARRIAGE

PRESIDENT SPENCER W. KIMBALL

&DIVORCE

© 1976 by Deseret Book Company
All rights reserved
ISBN 0-87747-635-7
Library of Congress Catalog Card No. 76-49802
Printed in the United States of America

Through the years I have warned the youth of Zion against the sins and vices so prevalent in our society—those of sexual impurity and all of its many ugly approaches. I have spoken of immodesty in dress and actions as one of the softening processes of Lucifer.

I have spoken plainly, warning youth of the pitfalls of petting and of all the other perversions into which young men and young women sometimes fall. I have endeavored also to give hope to those who might have stepped over the bounds of propriety, and I have outlined to them the path by which total repentance might bring them to forgiveness.

I have warned the youth against the many hazards of interfaith marriage, and with all the power I possessed, I have warned young people to avoid the sorrows and disillusionments that come from marrying out of the Church and the unhappy situations that almost invariably result when a believer marries an unbelieving spouse. I have pointed out the demands of the Church upon its members in time, energy, and funds; the deepness of the spiritual ties that tighten after marriage and as the family comes; the antagonisms that naturally follow such mismating; and that these and many other reasons argue eloquently for marriage within the Church where husband and wife have common backgrounds, common ideals and standards, common beliefs, hopes and objectives, and above all, where marriage may be eternalized through righteous entry into the holy temple.

Now I wish to follow these important principles with a discussion of family life. This topic is not new nor is it spectacular, but it is vital.

*Love cannot be expected
to last forever unless it is continually
fed with portions of love,
the manifestation of esteem and admiration,
the expressions of gratitude,
and the consideration of unselfishness*

Marriage is relevant in every life, and family life is the basis of our existence. I make no apology for discussing this subject. The entertainer gives to the people that which they desire. But I, like Paul, am pressed in the spirit to warn and to strengthen. May I have the blessings of our Heavenly Father in my words.

The ugly dragon of divorce has entered into our social life. Little known to our grandparents and not even common among our parents, this cancer has come to be so common in our own day that nearly every family has been cursed by its destructive machinations. This is one of the principal tools of Satan to destroy faith, through breaking up happy homes and bringing frustration of life and distortion of thought.

Honorable, happy, and successful marriage is surely the principal goal of every normal person. One who would purposely or neglectfully avoid its serious implications is not only not normal, but is frustrating his own program. There are also a few people who marry for spite or marry for wealth or marry on the rebound after having been jilted. How distorted is the thinking of such a one!

Marriage is perhaps the most vital of all the decisions and has the most far-reaching effects, for it has to do not only with immediate happiness, but eternal joys as well. It affects not only the two people involved, but also their families and particularly their children and their children's children down through the many generations. It is absolutely appalling how many children today are growing up in our society who do not have two parents, a father and a mother—and neither one is totally sufficient, if two could be had.

In selecting a companion for life and for eternity, certainly the most careful planning and thinking and praying and fasting should be done to be sure that of all the decisions, this one must not be wrong. In true marriage there must be a union of minds as well as of hearts. Emotions must not wholly determine decisions, but the mind and the heart, strengthened by fasting and prayer and serious consideration, will give one a maximum chance of marital happiness.

Marriage is not easy; it is not simple, as evidenced by the ever-mounting divorce rate. Exact figures astound us. The following ones come from Salt Lake County, which are probably somewhere near average. There were 832 marriages in a single month, and there were 414 divorces. That is half as many divorces as marriages. There were 364 temple marriages and of the temple marriages, about 10 percent were dissolved by divorce. This is substantially better than the average, but we are chagrined that there should be *any* divorce following a temple marriage.

We are grateful that this one survey reveals that about 90 percent of the temple marriages hold fast. Because of this, we recommend that people marry those who are of the same racial background generally, and of somewhat the same economic and social and educational background. Some of these are not an absolute necessity, but preferred; and above all, the same religious background, without question. In spite of the most favorable matings, the evil one still takes a monumental toll and is the cause for many broken homes and frustrated lives.

With all conditions as nearly ideal as possible, there are still people who terminate their marriages for the reason of "incompatibility." We see so many movies and television programs and read so much fiction and come in contact with so many society scandals that the people in general come to think of "marrying and giving in marriage," divorcing and remarrying, as the normal patterns.

The divorce itself does not constitute the entire evil, but the very acceptance of divorce as a cure is also a serious sin of this generation. Because a program or a pattern is universally accepted is not evidence that it is right. Marriage never was easy. It may never be. It brings with it sacrifice, sharing, and a demand for great selflessness.

Many of the TV and movie screen shows and stories of fiction end with marriage, and "they lived happily ever after." Since nearly all of us have experienced divorce among our close friends or relatives, we have come to realize that divorce is not a cure for difficulty, but is merely an escape, and a weak one. We have come to realize also that the mere performance of a ceremony does not bring happiness and a successful marriage. Happiness does not come by pressing a button, as does the electric light; happiness is a state of mind and comes from within. It must be earned. It cannot be purchased with money; it cannot be taken for nothing.

Some think of happiness as a glamorous life of ease, luxury, and constant thrills; but true marriage is based on a happiness that is more than that, one that comes from giving, serving, sharing, sacrificing, and selflessness.

Two people coming from different

backgrounds soon learn after the ceremony is performed that stark reality must be faced. There is no longer a life of fantasy or of make-believe; we must come out of the clouds and put our feet firmly on the earth. Responsibility must be assumed and new duties must be accepted. Some personal freedoms must be relinquished and many adjustments, unselfish adjustments, must be made.

One comes to realize very soon after marriage that the spouse has weaknesses not previously revealed or discovered. The virtues that were constantly magnified during courtship now grow relatively smaller, and the weaknesses that seemed so small and insignificant during courtship now grow to sizeable proportions. The hour has come for understanding hearts, for self-appraisal, and for good common sense, reasoning, and planning. The habits of years now show themselves; the spouse may be stingy or prodigal, lazy or industrious, devout or irreligious, kind and cooperative or petulant and cross, demanding or giving, egotistical or self-effacing. The in-law problem comes closer into focus and the relationship of the spouses to them is again magnified.

Often there is an unwillingness to settle down and assume the heavy responsibilities that immediately are there. Economy is reluctant to replace lavish living, and the young people seem often too eager "to keep up with the Joneses." There is often an unwillingness to make the necessary financial adjustments. Young wives often demand that all the luxuries formerly enjoyed in the prosperous homes of their successful fathers be continued in their own home. Some of

*Divorce is not a cure
for difficulty, but is merely
an escape, and a weak one.
We have come to realize also that
the mere performance of a ceremony
does not bring happiness and a
successful marriage. Happiness does not
come by pressing a button,
as does the electric light; happiness
is a state of mind and comes from within.
It must be earned. It cannot
be purchased with money;
it cannot be taken for nothing*

TREVOR SOUTHEY

them are quite willing to help earn that lavish living by continuing employment after marriage. They consequently leave the home, where their duty lies, to pursue professional or business pursuits, thus establishing an economy that becomes stabilized so that it becomes very difficult to yield toward the normal family life. With both spouses working, competition rather than cooperation enters the family. Two weary workers return home with taut nerves, individual pride, and increased independence, and then misunderstandings arise. Little frictions pyramid into monumental ones. Frequently, spouses sinfully turn to old romances or take up new ones, and finally the seemingly inevitable break comes with a divorce, with its heartaches, bitterness, disillusionment, and always scars.

While marriage is difficult, and discordant and frustrated marriages are common, yet real, lasting happiness is possible, and marriage can be more an exultant ecstasy than the human mind can conceive. This is within the reach of every couple, every person. "Soulmates" are fiction and an illusion; and while every young man and young woman will seek with all diligence and prayerfulness to find a mate with whom life can be most compatible and beautiful, yet it is certain that almost any good man and any good woman can have happiness and a successful marriage if both are willing to pay the price.

There is a never-failing formula that will guarantee to every couple a happy and eternal marriage; but like all formulas, the principal ingredients must not be left out, reduced, nor limited. The selection before courting and then the continued courting after the marriage process are equally important, but not more important than the marriage itself, the success of which depends upon the two individuals—not upon one, but upon two.

When a couple have commenced a marriage based upon reasonable standards, no combination of power can destroy that marriage except the power within either or both of the spouses themselves; and they must assume the responsibility generally. Other people and agencies may influence for good or bad; financial, social, political, and other situations may seem to have a bearing. But the marriage depends first and always on the two spouses, who can always make their marriage successful and happy if they are determined, unselfish, and righteous.

The formula is simple; the ingredients are few, though there are many amplifications of each.

First, there must be the proper approach toward marriage, which contemplates the selection of a spouse who reaches as nearly as possible the pinnacle of perfection in all the matters that are of importance to the individuals. Then those two parties must come to the altar in the temple realizing that they must work hard toward this successful joint living.

Second, there must be great unselfishness, forgetting self and directing all of the family life and all pertaining thereunto to the good of the family, and subjugating self.

Third, there must be continued courting and expressions of affection, kindness, and consideration to keep love alive and growing.

Fourth, there must be complete living of the commandments of the Lord as defined in the gospel of Jesus Christ.

With these ingredients properly mixed and continually kept functioning, it is quite impossible for unhappiness to come, for misunderstandings to continue, or for breaks to occur. Divorce attorneys would need to transfer to other fields and divorce courts would be padlocked.

Two individuals approaching the marriage altar must realize that in order for them to attain the happy marriage they hope for, they must know that marriage is not a legal cover-all. Rather, it means sacrifice, sharing, and even a reduction of some personal liberties. It means long, hard economizing. It means children who bring with them financial burdens, service burdens, care and worry burdens; but also it means the deepest and sweetest emotions of all.

Before marriage, each individual is quite free to go and come as he pleases, to organize and plan his life as it seems best; to make all decisions with self as the central point. Sweethearts should realize before they take the vows that each must accept literally and fully that the good of the new little family must always be superior to the good of either spouse. Each party must eliminate the "I" and the "my" and substitute therefor "we" and "our." Every decision must take into consideration that now two or more are affected by it. As she approaches major decisions now, the wife will be concerned as to the effect they will have upon the parents, the children, the home, and their spiritual lives. The husband's choice of occupation, his social life, his friends, his every interest must now be considered in the light that he is only a part of a family, that the totalness of the group must be considered.

Every divorce is the result of selfishness on the part of one or the other or both parties to a marriage contract. Someone is thinking of self-comforts, conveniences, freedoms, luxuries, or ease. Sometimes the ceaseless pinpricking of an unhappy, discontented, and selfish spouse can finally add up to serious physical violence. Sometimes people are goaded to the point where they erringly feel justified in doing the things that are so wrong. Nothing, of course, justifies sin.

Sometimes the husband or the wife feels neglected, mistreated, and ignored until he or she wrongly feels justified in adding to errors. If each spouse submits to frequent self-analysis and measures his own imperfections by the yardstick of perfection and the Golden Rule, and if each spouse sets about to correct self in every deviation found by such analysis rather than to set about to correct the deviations in the other party, then transformation comes and happiness is the result. There are many pharisaic people who marry who should memorize the parable of the Savior in Luke—people who prate their own virtues and pile up their own qualities of goodness and put them on the scales against the weaknesses of the spouse. They say, "I fast twice a week; I give tithes of all I possess." (See Luke 18:9-14.)

For every friction, there is a cause; and whenever there is unhappiness, each should search self to find the cause or at least that portion of the cause which originated in that self.

A marriage may not always be even and incident-less, but it can be one of great peace. A couple may have poverty, illness, disappointment, failures, and even death in the family, but even these will not rob them of their peace. The

19

*Marriage is not
a legal coverall. Rather,
it means sacrifice, sharing,
and even a reduction of some personal
liberties. It means long,
hard economizing. It means children
who bring with them financial burdens,
service burdens, care and worry burdens;
but also it means the deepest
and sweetest emotions of all*

marriage can be successful so long as selfishness does not enter in. Troubles and problems will draw parents together into unbreakable unions if there is total unselfishness there. During the depression of the 1930s there was a definite drop in divorce. Poverty, failures, disappointment—they tied parents together. Adversity can cement relationships that prosperity can destroy.

The marriage that is based upon selfishness is almost certain to fail. The one who marries for wealth or the one who marries for prestige or social plane is certain to be disappointed. The one who marries to satisfy vanity and pride or who marries to spite or to show up another person is fooling only himself. But the one who marries to give happiness as well as receive it, to give service as well as to receive it, and looks after the interests of the two and then the family as it comes will have a good chance that the marriage will be a happy one.

There are many people who do not find divorce attorneys and who do not end their marriages, but who have permitted their marriage to grow stale and weak and cheap. There are spouses who have fallen from the throne of adoration and worship and are in the low state of mere joint occupancy of the home, joint sitters at the table, joint possessors of certain things that cannot be easily divided. These people are on the path that leads to trouble. These people will do well to reevaluate, to renew their courting, to express their affection, to acknowledge kindnesses, and to increase their consideration so their marriage can again become beautiful, sweet, and growing.

Love is like a flower, and, like the body, it

needs constant feeding. The mortal body would soon be emaciated and die if there were not frequent feedings. The tender flower would wither and die without food and water. And so love, also, cannot be expected to last forever unless it is continually fed with portions of love, the manifestation of esteem and admiration, the expressions of gratitude, and the consideration of unselfishness.

Total unselfishness is sure to accomplish another factor in successful marriage. If each spouse is forever seeking the interests, comforts, and happiness of the other, the love found in courtship and cemented in marriage will grow into mighty proportions. Many couples permit their marriages to become stale and their love to grow cold like old bread or worn-out jokes or cold gravy. Certainly the foods most vital for love are consideration, kindness, thoughtfulness, concern, expressions of affection, embraces of appreciation, admiration, pride, companionship, confidence, faith, partnership, equality, and dependence.

To be really happy in marriage, there must be a continued faithful observance of the commandments of the Lord. No one, single or married, was ever sublimely happy unless he was righteous. There are temporary satisfactions and camouflaged situations for the moment, but permanent, total happiness can come only through cleanliness and worthiness. One who has a pattern of religious life with deep religious convictions can never be happy in an inactive life. The conscience will continue to afflict unless it has been seared, in which case the marriage is already in jeopardy. A stinging conscience can make life most unbearable. Inactivity is destructive to marriage, especially where the parties are inactive in varying degrees. Religious differences are the most trying and among the most unsolvable of all differences.

Marriage is ordained of God. It is not merely a social custom. Without proper and successful marriage, one will never be exalted. Read the words of the Lord, that it is right and proper to be married.

This being true, the thoughtful, intelligent Latter-day Saint will plan his life carefully to be sure there are no impediments placed in the way. To make one serious mistake, one may place in the way obstacles that may never be removed and that may block the way to eternal life and godhood—our ultimate destiny. If two people love the Lord more than their own lives and then love each other more than their own lives, working together in total harmony with the gospel program as their basic structure, they are sure to have this great happiness. When a husband and wife go together frequently to the holy temple, kneel in prayer together in their home with their family, go hand in hand to their religious meetings, keep their lives wholly chaste, mentally and physically, so that their whole thoughts and desires and love are all centered in one being, their companion, and both are working together for the upbuilding of the kingdom of God, then happiness is at its pinnacle.

Sometimes in marriage there are other cleavings, in spite of the fact that the Lord said, "Thou shalt love thy wife with all thy heart, and shalt cleave unto her and none else." (D&C 42:22.)

This means just as completely that "thou shalt love thy *husband* with all thy heart and shall cleave unto *him* and none else." Frequently, people continue to cleave unto their mothers and their fathers and their friends. Sometimes mothers will not relinquish the hold they have had upon their children, and husbands as well as wives return to their mothers and fathers for advice and counsel and to confide; whereas cleaving should be to the wife or husband in most things, and all intimacies should be kept in great secrecy and privacy from others.

Couples do well to immediately find their own home, separate and apart from that of the in-laws on either side. The home may be very modest and unpretentious, but still it is an independent domicile. Their married life should become independent of her folks and his folks. The couple love their parents more than ever; they cherish their counsel; they appreciate their association; but they must live their own lives, being governed by their own decisions, by their own prayerful considerations after they have received the counsel from those who should give it. To cleave does not mean merely to occupy the same home; it means to adhere closely, to stick together.

"Wherefore, it is lawful that . . . they twain shall be one flesh, and all this that the earth might answer the end of its creation;

"And that it might be filled with the measure of man, according to his creation before the world was made." (D&C 49:16-17.)

Our own record is not pleasing. Of 31,037 recent marriages, our records say only 14,169 were in the temple for eternity. This is 46 percent.

Some think of happiness
as a glamorous life of ease, luxury,
and constant thrills; but
true marriage is based on a happiness
that is more than that, one that
comes from giving, serving, sharing,
sacrificing, and selflessness

There were 7,556 members married out of the Church. This is terribly disturbing to us. This is 24 percent, which means that about 9,000, or 30 percent, apparently thought so little of themselves and their posterity that they married out of the temple, which could give them a key to eternal life. Is it possible they do not know or do they not care?

Of course, most such people who marry out of the Church and temple do not weigh the matter sufficiently. The survey I mentioned disclosed the fact that only about one out of seven would be converted and baptized into the Church. This is a great loss. It means that in many cases there is not only loss of the unbaptized spouse, but also of the children and even sometimes the other spouse.

We love those few who join the Church after marriage. We praise them and honor them, but the odds are against this happening. According to the figures given above, this means that nearly 6,500 of the new marriages may never find both parties finally joining the Church to make the family totally united. This grieves us very much. The total program of the Lord for the family cannot be enjoyed fully if the people are unequally yoked in marriage.

We call upon all youth to make such a serious, strong resolution to have a temple marriage that their determination will provide for them the rich promises of eternal marriage with its accompanying joys and happiness. This would please the Lord, who counts on each of us so heavily. He has said that eternal life can be had only in the way he has planned it.

"And a white stone is given to each of those who come into the celestial kingdom, whereon is a new name written, which no man knoweth save he that receiveth it. The new name is the key word." (D&C 130:11.)

It is the *normal* thing to marry. It was arranged by God in the beginning. One is not wholly normal who does not want to be married. Remember, ". . . neither is the man without the woman, neither the woman without the man, in the Lord." (1 Corinthians 11:11.)

No one can reject this covenant of celestial marriage and reach the eternal kingdom of God. This is certain.

"In the celestial glory there are three heavens or degrees;

"And in order to obtain the highest, a man must enter into this order of the priesthood [meaning the new and everlasting covenant of marriage];

"And if he does not, he cannot obtain it.

"He may enter into the other, but that is the end of his kingdom. . . ." (D&C 131:1-4.)

"For behold, I reveal unto you a new and everlasting covenant; and if ye abide not that covenant, then are ye damned. . . ." (D&C 132:4.) And damned means stopped in progress.

These are the words of the Lord. They were said directly to us. There is no question about them.

"And as pertaining to the new and everlasting covenant, it was instituted for the fulness of my glory; and he that receiveth a fulness thereof must and shall abide the law. . . .

"Therefore, when they are out of the world [after they have died] they neither marry nor are given in marriage; but are appointed angels in heaven; which angels are ministering servants, to minister for those who are worthy of a far more, and an exceeding, and an eternal weight of glory.

"For these angels did not abide my law; therefore, they cannot be enlarged, but remain separately and singly, without exaltation, in their saved condition, to all eternity; and from henceforth are not gods, but are angels of God forever and ever.

"Abraham received all things, whatsoever he received, by revelation and commandment, by my word, saith the Lord, and hath entered into his exaltation and sitteth upon his throne.

"Go ye, therefore, and do the works of Abraham; enter ye into my law and ye shall be saved." (D&C 132:6, 16-17, 29, 32.)

This is the word of the Lord. It is very, very serious, and there is nobody who should argue with the Lord. He made the earth; he made the people. He knows the conditions. He set the program, and we are not intelligent enough or smart enough to be able to argue him out of these important things. He knows what is right and true.

We ask each Latter-day Saint to think of these things. Be sure that your marriage is right. Be sure that your life is right. Be sure that your part of the marriage is carried forward properly.

Now I ask the Lord to bless you. These things worry us considerably because there are too many divorces and they are increasing. It has come to be a common thing to talk about divorce. The minute there is a little crisis or a little argument in the family, we talk about divorce, and we rush to see an attorney. This is not the way of the Lord. We should go back and adjust our problems and make our marriage compatible and sweet and blessed.

I pray the Lord will bless each one who faces decisions before marriage and after marriage. I ask his blessings upon each one of you and give you my testimony that this church is true and divine, in the name of Jesus Christ. Amen.

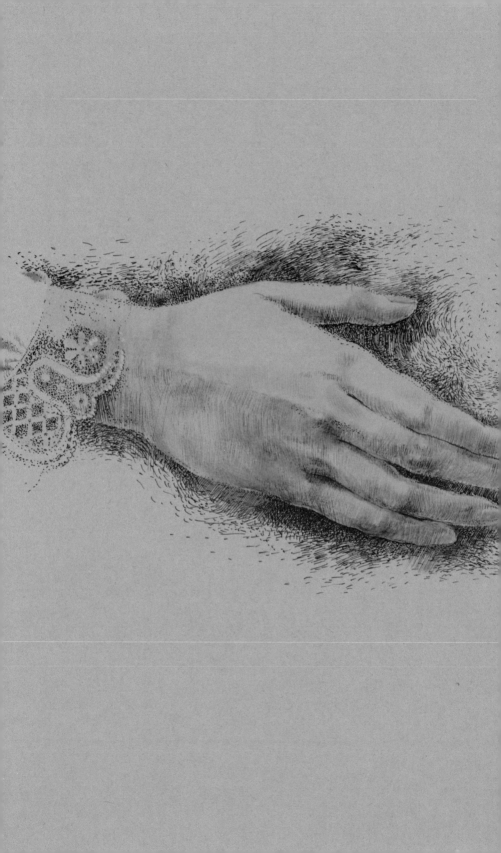